MAR 0 9

Smart Animals

WHALES

by Lisa Rao

Consultant: Jenny Montague
Assistant Curator of Marine Mammals
New England Aquarium
Boston, MA

BEARPORT
PUBLISHING

New York, New York

Credits

Cover, © James D. Watt/SeaPics.com and Doug Perrine/SeaPics.com; Title Page, © James D. Watt/SeaPics.com; 4, © AP Images/Jeff David; 5, © Andrea Mohin/The New York Times/Redux; 6L, © 2004 Kike Calvo/V&W/Image Quest Marine; 6R, © Brandon Cole Marine Photography/Alamy; 8, © Todd Pusser/SeaPics.com; 9L, © 2007 Mark Conlin/V&W/Image Quest Marine; 9R, © David Tipling/Nature Picture Library; 10L, © Michael S. Nolan/SeaPics.com; 10R, © 2007 Kike Calvo/V&W/Image Quest Marine; 11, © Duncan Murrell/SeaPics.com; 12, © Doug Perrine/SeaPics.com; 13, © James D. Watt/SeaPics.com; 14, © D. Parer & E. Parer-Cook/AUSCAPE/Minden Pictures; 15, © Masa Ushioda/SeaPics.com; 16, © Flip Nicklin/Minden Pictures; 17, © Hiroya Minakuchi/SeaPics.com; 18, © Flip Nicklin/Science Faction/Getty Images; 19, © Jonathan Bird/Peter Arnold Inc.; 21L, © Jean Paul Ferrero/Ardea.com; 21R, © Masa Ushioda/Stephen Frink Collection /Alamy; 22, © Lin Sutherland/SeaPics.com; 23, © Brandon Cole/BIOS/Peter Arnold Inc; 24, © 2006 Danny Frank/Image Quest Marine; 25, © Hiroya Minakuchi/SeaPics.com; 26, © Mark Spencer/Ardea.com; 27, © Michael S. Nolan/SeaPics.com; 28L, © Masa Ushioda/SeaPics.com; 28R, © Doc White/Nature Picture Library; 29, © The Whale Center of New England.

Publisher: Kenn Goin
Editorial Director: Adam Siegel
Creative Director: Spencer Brinker
Original Design: Dawn Beard Creative
Photo Researcher: Amy Dunleavy

Special thanks to Martha Hiatt

Library of Congress Cataloging-in-Publication Data

Rao, Lisa.
 Whales / by Lisa Rao.
     p. cm. — (Smart animals!)
 Includes bibliographical references and index.
 ISBN-13: 978-1-59716-579-2 (library binding)
 ISBN-10: 1-59716-579-4 (library binding)
 1. Whales—Juvenile literature. 2. Whales—Psychology—Juvenile literature. I. Title.

 QL737.C4R24 2008
 599.5'15—dc22

                              2007039709

For more information, write to Bearport Publishing Company, Inc., 101 Fifth Avenue, Suite 6R, New York, New York 10003. Printed in the United States of America.

10 9 8 7 6 5 4 3 2 1

Contents

Keeping a Clean Home

It was night at the New York **Aquarium**. Kathy was not asleep, however. She was hunting for objects that had fallen into her pool. Maybe she'd spot a tiny rock or a leaf. Kathy was smart. She knew that if she found something, she would get a special treat.

▲ **Visitors at the aquarium enjoyed watching Kathy.**

In the morning, Kathy would race over to her **trainers** and open her mouth. On her tongue was one of the small objects she had found.

"We'd call it a gift from Kathy," said Martha Hiatt, a trainer at the aquarium where Kathy lived. As a **reward** for finding something, Kathy's trainers would give her a fish—the perfect snack for a beluga whale!

Scientists believe that whales are among the smartest animals in the world.

▲ **Martha and Kathy**

Listening for Food

There are about 80 kinds of whales. Most of them, including belugas like Kathy, have teeth. They use them to catch fish, squid, octopus, and other **prey**. It's often hard to see in the dark ocean water, however. So how do these clever animals find their food?

▲ Toothed whales, such as belugas (top) and killer whales (right), do not chew their food. Instead, they tear off pieces of their prey and then gulp them down.

Most toothed whales use clicking sounds. They aim the clicks with the large, rounded part of their heads called the melon. The sounds bounce off objects and return to the whales. The bouncing sound is called an **echo**. Toothed whales use the echoes to tell the size, shape, and distance of their prey.

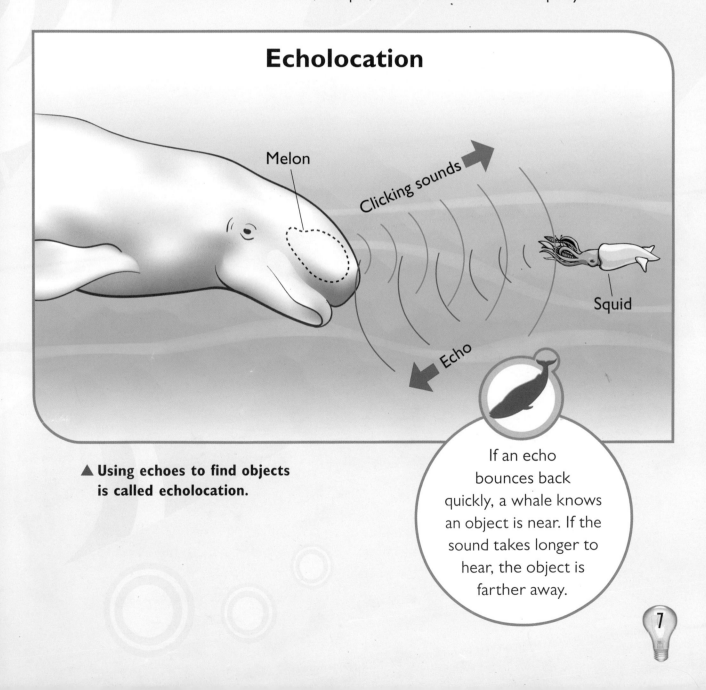

Echolocation

Melon

Clicking sounds

Squid

Echo

▲ **Using echoes to find objects is called echolocation.**

If an echo bounces back quickly, a whale knows an object is near. If the sound takes longer to hear, the object is farther away.

Taking a Big Gulp

Some kinds of whales do not have teeth. Instead, they have hundreds of long, thin plates in their mouth called **baleen**. These kinds of whales do not use echoes to find food. They use their baleen to catch fish and millions of tiny animals called **krill**. How?

▲ Baleen hangs down from a whale's upper jaw, as seen on this gray whale. Baleen is made of the same kind of material as a person's fingernails.

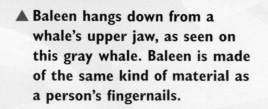

There are two main groups of whales— toothed whales and baleen whales. Toothed whales include belugas, killer whales, and sperm whales. Baleen whales include blue whales, gray whales, and humpbacks.

First, a baleen whale opens its mouth. It takes in big gulps of water where fish and krill are swimming. Then the whale shuts its mouth. It squeezes the water out through the strips of baleen. Only the fish and krill are left behind. The hungry whale can now swallow its food.

▲ A close-up of krill

▲ There are more than 90 kinds of krill. They range in size from about .5 inches (1 cm) to 6 inches (15 cm) long.

Bubbles and Slams

Humpback whales are a kind of baleen whale. They catch their prey in a clever way. First, they dive under a group of fish. Then they swim up in a circle. As they swim, they blow air bubbles out of their **blowholes**, the two holes on top of their heads. The bubbles form a net around the fish and trap them. The whales can then swim right up and eat them!

▲ These humpback whales are swimming in a circle to make a bubble net that will trap fish.

▲ A humpback whale's blowholes

In 1981, scientists were studying a humpback whale named Molson. They were amazed by what they saw. Molson had found a smart, new way to trap fish. Before blowing any bubbles, Molson jumped out of the ocean and slammed her chin and tail on the water. Then she dived below to make a bubble net where she had slammed. The scientists thought Molson used her body slams to **stun** the fish before she trapped them with her bubbles.

▲ **A group of humpbacks feeding on the fish they have trapped**

Sometimes just one humpback will make a bubble net. Often, however, a group of humpbacks will do it. Then all the whales get to eat the trapped fish. Working together is a smart way to feed everyone.

Follow the Leader

Molson's body slams led to a big surprise. Soon, many other whales in the ocean were also slamming their tails and bodies to catch fish. Scientists think the whales were copying Molson.

▲ **A humpback whale slamming its tail on the water**

Copying is a sign of an **intelligent** animal. When animals copy one another, it means they are learning from one another.

Baby whales, called **calves**, often copy the actions of their mothers. One time a baby killer whale watched her mother do jumps around a pool. The mother had been trained to do this. At first the calf just watched. After a while, however, the calf started to do small jumps next to her. Soon she was doing the same jumps as her mother all the way around the tank. The calf hadn't been trained. She had just watched her mother and copied her.

▲ These killer whales have been trained to jump out of the water.

Watching and Learning

Some young whales learn to hunt by copying the actions of adults. For example, killer whales show their young how to attack sea lions on a beach. First the adults **lunge** toward the sand. Then they roll aside and let their young practice the same movement.

▲ **A killer whale trying to catch sea lions**

Many smart animals, such as whales, sea lions, and orangutans, learn to do things by watching the actions of their parents or other adults.

Whales don't just copy actions. They also copy sounds. At one aquarium, trainers who were working with beluga whales would blow a whistle to let them know they had done something right. Then the whales would get a treat. One beluga learned to make the sound of the whistle. When he did, the other whales stopped working and waited for their treat!

▲ Beluga whales can make more than 15 different kinds of clicks and whistles.

Teamwork

Scientists say that hunting in a group is another sign of intelligent animals. Beluga whales live in groups called **pods**. One pod may have up to 25 whales in it. The belugas use teamwork to catch their food. First the whales circle a group of fish. Then they force the fish into shallow water and eat them.

▲ **A pod of beluga whales**

Whales in a pod often slap their tails on the water. Scientists think they make noisy splashes to tell other whales in the pod where they are.

Killer whales also hunt in pods. Most of these animals are between 20 and 30 feet (6 and 9 m) long. Yet scientists once saw a pod of 30 killer whales go after a 60-foot (18-m) blue whale. The killer whales circled their prey on all sides so it couldn't escape. Then they attacked as a group. By hunting together, the killer whales were able to kill an animal that was bigger than themselves.

▲ **Killer whales are the only kind of whale that will attack other whales.**

Safety in Numbers

Whales work together to hunt. They also stay together to keep safe. One time, scientists were watching a pod of sperm whales in the ocean. Suddenly, a group of killer whales began surrounding them. To stay safe, the sperm whales formed a circle. They turned their bodies to face the killer whales. As a group, the sperm whales kept their big square heads facing out and their tails and bodies in the center of the circle.

▲ **A pod of sperm whales**

For three hours, the killer whales tried to swim behind the sperm whales to attack them. Yet the sperm whales stayed close together in a circle. Eventually, the killer whales gave up and swam away.

Scientists have found that smart animals tend to be **social**. They live in groups where they work together and help one another stay safe.

▲ A sperm whale's giant head is about 20 feet (6 m) long. It makes up more than one third of its body.

Finding a Warm Home

Many baleen whales, such as humpbacks and gray whales, travel far together as a group. In the winter, parts of the ocean get very cold. So in the fall, the whales swim, or **migrate**, to places where the ocean water is warmer. They spend the winter there.

Where humpback whales travel in the fall

Humpback whales migrate farther than any other kind of whale. Some swim more than 5,100 miles (8,208 km) from the cold ocean around Antarctica to warm waters in Central America.

Once females have reached the warm water, they give birth to their babies. By late spring, it is time for the whales and their young to return home. Their trip can take several months. Scientists still aren't exactly sure how the whales find their way back.

▲ **Migrating humpback whales**

Caring for Calves

Whale mothers often live together in groups with their calves. It's a smart way to make sure that their young stay safe. When one mother swims off to find food, another mother will babysit her calf. She keeps it safe from sharks and other **predators**.

▲ **Adult sperm whales and calf**

Sometimes an experienced mother whale will help out a new mother. At the New York Aquarium, a mother beluga lived with a younger female that had just had a baby. The younger mother didn't know how to care for her calf. So the older female helped teach her.

▲ **A mother beluga whale and her calf**

Being able to teach and pass on information is a sign of a smart animal.

Taking a Peek

Scientists have found that smart animals are often curious. Beacon was a humpback that would raise her head straight up out of the ocean and take a quick look around. Then she would slip back down into the water. This action is called spyhopping.

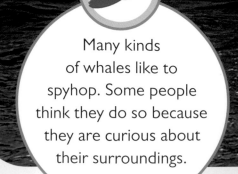

Many kinds of whales like to spyhop. Some people think they do so because they are curious about their surroundings.

STAR OF MONTER

▲ **A humpback whale spyhopping**

Beacon wasn't shy about spyhopping. Often she would swim near people, raise her head, and stare right at them. She was as curious about them as they were about her!

▲ **Killer whales spyhopping**

25

More to Learn

Scientists have learned a lot about whales by watching and working with them. Yet many of the things that whales do are still puzzling. Some whales, such as humpbacks, leap out of the water and then fall back with a big splash. This action is called breaching. Do whales do it to show off or to have fun? No one knows for sure.

▲ A humpback whale breaching

Scientists also wonder why whales make noises that sound like songs. Are they communicating with one another in the water? Are they trying to attract a **mate**? Scientists cannot say for certain. There is still much more to learn about these smart and amazing creatures.

Scientists are able to identify different humpback whales by looking at the markings on their tails.

Just the Facts

Humpback Whale

Beluga Whale

	Humpback Whale		Beluga Whale
Type	baleen whale	**Type**	toothed whale
Weight	50,000–80,000 pounds (23,000–36,000 kg)	**Weight**	about 2,000 pounds (900 kg)
Length	45–50 feet (14–15 m)	**Length**	10–15 feet (3–4.5 m)
Food	mainly small fish and krill	**Food**	mainly fish, squid, crabs, and shrimp
Habitat	all oceans	**Habitat**	icy waters of the Arctic and nearby seas
Predators	killer whales	**Predators**	polar bears and killer whales

More Smart Whales

In 1990, Humphrey, a humpback whale, got stuck in San Francisco Bay. Scientists were able to lead him back to the ocean by using two groups of boats. One group stayed behind the whale, and the other stayed in front. People behind Humphrey banged on steel pipes to make loud, ugly noises. People in front played a recording of humpback songs. Humphrey was smart enough to follow the pretty whale music to the ocean!

Silver was a female humpback that taught scientists about whale friendship. Humpbacks often form groups that stay together for about a day. In 1979, 1982, and 1984, however, Silver was often seen with the same female humpback named T-Square. Both whales were pregnant at those times. In years when they were not pregnant, the whales were never seen together.

◀ **Half of Silver's tail was missing. It had been cut off, probably by the sharp blade of a boat.**

Glossary

aquarium (uh-KWAIR-ee-uhm) a building with large tanks or pools where people can see different kinds of sea creatures

baleen (buh-LEEN) long, thin plates inside a whale's mouth used to separate small animals out of the water for food

blowholes (BLOH-hohlz) the openings on top of a whale's head that allow the animal to take in and let out air

calves (KAVS) baby whales

echo (EK-oh) a sound that bounces off an object and returns to the place that it came from

intelligent (in-TEL-uh-juhnt) smart

krill (KRIL) tiny shrimp-like animals that live in the ocean

lunge (LUHNJ) to move forward quickly and without warning

mate (MATE) one of a pair of animals that have young together

migrate (MYE-grate) to move from one place to another at a certain time of the year

pods (PODZ) groups of whales that live together

predators (PRED-uh-turz) animals that hunt other animals for food

prey (PRAY) animals that are hunted or caught for food

reward (ri-WORD) what a person or animal gets for doing something useful or good

social (SOH-shuhl) living in groups and having contact with others

stun (STUN) to shock something so much that it is unable to move

trainers (TRAYN-urz) people who teach animals or other people to do something

Bibliography

D'Vincent, Cynthia. *The Whale Family Book.* Saxonville, MA: Picture Book Studio (1992).

Hoyt, Erich. *Meeting the Whales.* Ontario, Canada: Camden House (1991).

Lauber, Patricia. *Great Whales: The Gentle Giants.* New York: Scholastic (1991).

Papastavrou, Vassili. *Whale.* New York: DK Publishing (2004).

Read More

Esbensen, Barbara Juster. *Baby Whales Drink Milk.* New York: HarperCollins (1994).

Simon, Seymour. *Whales.* New York: HarperCollins (2006).

Squire, Ann O. *Beluga Whales.* Danbury, CT: Children's Press (2007).

Thomson, Sarah L. *Amazing Whales!* New York: HarperCollins (2005).

Wolpert, Tom. *Whales for Kids.* Minnetonka, MN: NorthWord Press (2000).

Learn More Online

To learn more about whales, visit
www.bearportpublishing.com/SmartAnimals

31

Index

About the Author

Lisa Rao has written more than a dozen books for children. When she's not reading or writing, she enjoys swimming and rooting for the New York Mets.